Grammar St

Contents

unit 1

Sentence construction 1

All sentences need a verb.

A verb is an "action word" or a "doing word".

>Tariq played the drums.

Played is the verb, it is what Tariq was **doing**.

A verb can also be a "being" word. It tells you what someone or something is.

>Tariq is a boy.

The verb **is** tells us that Tariq **is** a boy.

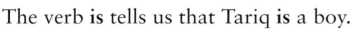 **Try it out!**

Here is a list of words. Ten of them are verbs. Write the ten hidden verbs into your book. *(1 mark for each correct answer)*

The man can…

play	boy	walk	run	dance	throw	pink	baby
hear	write	shout	eat	clock	card	jump	

Read these ten sentences and find the verb in each one. Write each sentence in your book underlining the verb. Tariq <u>threw</u> the ball. *(1 mark for each correct answer)*

1   Tariq plays the drums.
2   The man hit the ball.
3   The frog is green.
4   Tariq ran in the race.
5   Mary sang a song.
6   Tariq's house is very old.
7   Miss Jones waved to Tariq.
8   Mary and Tariq swam in the pool.
9   The man cut his lawn.
10 Miss Jones ticked Tariq's Maths book.

Write a sentence using each of these verbs.

(1 mark for each correct answer)

| 1 play | 2 hop | 3 eat | 4 sleep | 5 walk |
| 6 stir | 7 talk | 8 laugh | 9 rub | 10 press |

You may want to start your sentences with "I" followed by the verb. For example:

   I play the drums. *(1 mark for each correct answer)*

Sentence construction 2

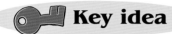 Key idea

A sentence is a group of words which tells us something. Sentences must make sense!

- **Amy shoes walked park.** This is not a sentence. It does not carry an idea. It does not make sense.

- **Amy got some new shoes. Amy walked to the park.** These sentences tell us something. They carry an idea. They do make sense.

- Each sentence you write should tell the reader something and make sense.

Try it out!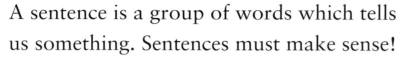

Some of these sentences do not make sense. Write out the five REAL sentences into your book. *(2 marks for each correct answer)*

1 I had a hot bath.
2 The dog ran after Tariq.
3 The dog cards Tuesday.
4 I ate a bar of chocolate.
5 Move sun tries band.

6 The cup was broken.
7 Amy flew grand watch.
8 Tariq quickly has blowing.
9 The cat spark shed clean.
10 The hen laid an egg.

The words in these sentences are in the wrong order. Rewrite each sentence into your book, so that it makes sense. *(1 mark for each correct answer)*

1 The barks. dog
2 I in the garden. play
3 washed the Dad car.
4 busy. The shop was
5 is wind The blowing.

6 ball. I the hit
7 was hat The red.
8 Amy eggs. the fried
9 toast The hot. was
10 asleep. cat The was

These sentences do not make sense. There is a mistake in each one. Copy the sentences into your book and correct each one. *(1 mark for each correct answer)*

1 Amy combed her face.
2 The doctor comed to help.
3 Adam went to visit Amys.
4   Amy ate some milk.
5 The fish swam by the water.
6 Amy opened her mouths to sing.
7 Tariq and Amy plays in the park.
8 Adam did not fill well.
9 The sun was cold.
10 Tariq had not catched a fish all day.

Sentence construction 3

 **Key idea**

All sentences have a subject and an object.

The **subject** tells us "who" or "what" the sentence is about. The subject goes with the verb. The **object** of a sentence is the person or thing the subject is doing something to.

> Amy kicked the ball.

- Amy is the **subject**, as she kicked the ball.
- The ball is the **object** because Amy kicked it.

Try it out! ●

Write out the subject from each of these sentences. Make a list of the subjects in your book. *(1 mark for each correct answer)*

1 John hid the book.
2 Amy sang a song.
3 The teacher was cross with the boy.
4 Tariq picked up the ball.
5 The doctor looked in Amy's ear.
6 The painter finished the picture.
7 Tariq brushed his teeth.
8 Amy stirred the cake mixture.
9 John closed the door.
10 Amy washed her hair.

Read these sentences and pick out the object of the sentence.
Make a list of them in your book. *(1 mark for each correct answer)*
"John closed the door" – The door is the object as John is
closing it.

1 Adam threw the ball.   6 Amy opened her umbrella.
2 The dog sat on the mat.   7 The lady ate a large cake.
3 Tariq watched the baby.   8 The magician waved a wand.
4 Amy opened the can.   9 The teacher read the book.
5 Amy danced for the crowd. 10 Jake cut the grass.

The subject and object of each sentence have got mixed up!
Write out the sentences with the subject and object in the right
order. *(1 mark for each correct answer)*

1 The T.V. watched Tariq.
2 The tree ran around the dog.
3 A bag of crisps ate Amy.
4 The lemonade drank Tariq.
5 The homework marked the teacher.
6 The door locked Adam.
7 The egg laid a hen.
8 The bacon cooked Mum.
9 The letter posted Amy.
10 A book read Adam.

unit 4

Using full stops

 Key idea

A full stop marks the end of a sentence. It shows the reader where one idea ends.

Tariq likes fish and chips. He went to the shops on Saturday.

Two full stops are used, as there are two sentences.

Try it out! ●

Copy out these sentences. Put a full stop at the end of each one.

(1 mark for each correct answer)

1   Tariq was cross with Amy
2   The boy walked to school
3   The bird had a yellow beak
4   It was a sunny day
5   Amy played with Tariq
6   Adam had some crisps
7   The cat purred
8   The train was late
9   The curry was hot
10 The door was open

Copy out these pairs of sentences. Show the end of each sentence by adding a full stop. *(1 mark for each correct answer)*

For example:

John was tired. He went to bed.

1 Amy was hot Amy had a drink
2 The show was good Adam enjoyed it
3 John ate all of the cake He was full
4 Adam went shopping Adam got a toy boat
5 It was a cold day John put on his hat
6 The flowers were blue Amy picked some flowers to take home
7 The man went for a walk He walked to the park
8 Tariq did the washing up Tariq's mum was pleased
9 The girl was sad Her friend had moved house
10 Adam rang the bell The bell was loud

Take up the challenge! ····························

Copy out this short story into your book. Put in the full stops. There are ten to put in! *(1 mark for each correct answer)*

It was a sunny day Adam and Tariq went to the park They played on the swings Later they had an ice-cream It was lovely Amy arrived with her friend Jaswinda They all played together At 11 o'clock they all went home It had been a super morning They will meet again next week

unit 5 Capital letters

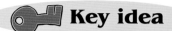

🔑 Key idea

Capital letters are used to show the start of a sentence and to identify proper nouns, such as names of people.

The clown looked funny. The clown's name was Freddy.

Each sentence starts with a capital letter and the clown's name, Freddy, begins with a capital letter too.

Try it out!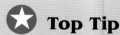

⭐ Top Tip

Don't forget that "I" is always a capital letter as it is a personal pronoun and stands for the writer's name!

Write out each sentence putting a capital letter at the start of the first word.

(1 mark for each correct answer)

1   on Tuesday I went to the circus.
2   i saw the clowns.
3   they were very funny.
4   the clowns had big red noses.
5   the show was for 1 hour.
6   i had an ice-cream.
7   there was a juggler too.
8   the tent was red and white.
9   they even had two fire-eaters.
10 it was really exciting.

There are two capital letters missing in each sentence. Write out the sentences putting in the missing capitals. *(1 mark for each correct answer)*

1   i saw my friend amit.
2   amit liked freddy the clown.
3   the clown called joey wore a red coat.
4   amit and i saw the whole show.
5   at the end, amit went home.

Take up the challenge ●●●●●●●●●●

!

ALERT
Remember there are TWO capital letters to find in each sentence! Check your work carefully!

Copy out this short story putting in the capital letters. *(1 mark for each correct answer)*

at the circus the clowns made a lot of mess. my favourite, freddy, threw pies at a clown called joey. freddy had big shoes which made amit and i laugh. he kept falling over them. joey threw a bucket of water at freddy!

Now write two short sentences of your own about the clowns. Remember to start each sentence with a capital letter.

unit 6 Word order in sentences

🔑 Key idea

A sentence must make sense. Each sentence has a subject and an object. Words in a sentence must be in the correct order.

    Landed on the grass a spaceship.

This sentence does not make sense. The word order is wrong.

    A spaceship landed on the grass.

This sentence does make sense. The words are in the correct order. The sentence tells us something, it conveys an idea.

Try it out! • • • • • • • • • • • • • • • •

Write out these sentences putting the words in the correct order. *(1 mark for each correct answer)*

1 a spaceship here landed.
2 silver was spaceship the.
3 big the was computer.
4 eyes had the red aliens
5 fingers they three had.
6 small feet had they.
7 hair their green was.
8 had big mouths they.
9 ears four they had.
10 no had they noses.

> ⭐ **Top Tip**
>
> Read your sentences carefully. Make sure each sentence makes sense. Remember to start each one with a capital letter!

The subject in each sentence of this news report is wrong. Write out the report changing the subject into the word "aliens". *(2 marks for each correct answer)*

For example: The cat flew the spaceship = The aliens flew the spaceship.

NEWSFLASH

The dogs have landed in Kent! Alligators have been seen with big mouths and red skin. Do not go near the bicycles if you see them. The fish could be dangerous. We believe the ladies have four ears and very small feet.

Take up the challenge! ···············

!

ALERT
Read back your report and make sure you have not missed out any words!

Complete the news report by writing some more facts about the aliens. *(2 marks for each correct sentence)*

The aliens' heads are…
Their toes…
They have only one…
The aliens' teeth…
Their…

Now write a short report about their spaceship.

Uses of capital letters

🔑 Key idea

Capital letters are used to show the start of a sentence, and to identify proper nouns – names of people, places, titles and times.

My friend **Adam**, who lives in **Kent**, will be seven in **May**.

- A sentence always starts with a capital letter.
- Adam is the name of a person, so it begins with a capital letter.
- Kent is the name of a place, so it begins with a capital letter.
- May is the name of a month, so it also begins with a capital letter.

Try it out!

Write out the words. Put in the capital letters at the start of each word. *(1 mark for each correct answer)*

monday	jane	ben	december	Friday	london
	amy	david	july	sunday	

14

There is a capital letter missing in each sentence. Find it and write the word correctly. *(1 mark for each correct answer)*

1 I have a friend called adam.
2 He lives in kent.
3 Adam had a day out in london.
4 His Auntie jane lives in Glasgow.
5 Adam goes to park Street School.
6 His teacher is called miss Jones.
7 blue is Adam's favourite colour.
8 Adam's best friend is called alex.
9 Adam goes swimming on mondays.
10 Last year Adam went to spain on holiday.

Find the ten mistakes in Adam's writing. Write it out, putting in the capital letters. *(1 mark for each correct answer)*

My name is adam and my birthday in on the tenth of may. For my birthday I would like to go to disneyland paris. I have a hamster whose name is george. His birthday is in june. I live in kent and I have two brothers called sam and paul. I also have a sister called anna.

Now make up two more sentences about Adam, using two capital letters in each sentence

Linking words

 Key idea

We can join short sentences together to make longer, more interesting sentences. We use link words like AND, SO or BUT.

> Amy went to the zoo. Amy saw lots of animals.
>
> = Amy went to the zoo and saw lots of animals.

We do not need the second "Amy" as we know she is the subject of the sentence.

Try it out!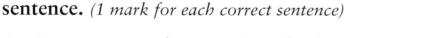

★ **Top Tip**
Remember there should only be one full stop at the end of the sentence.

Write out these pairs of sentences joining them with "and" to make one long sentence. *(1 mark for each correct sentence)*

1 Amy went to the zoo. Amy had a great time.
2 She saw lots of animals. She went around the whole zoo.
3 Amy went to Pet's Corner. Amy fed a rabbit.
4 It started to rain. It got very cold.
6 Amy ran for shelter. Amy hid under a tree.
7 Amy saw the lions. Amy was very scared.
8 She played on the swings. She slid down the slide.
9 Amy had some chips. Amy had a drink.
10 She bought a badge. She put it on.

Finish these sentences by adding more
information after the word "but".

ALERT
Remember to finish
each one with ideas
that match the start of
the sentences!

(2 marks for each sentence)

Amit was tired but he still went out to play.

1 Amy was wet but…
2 The elephants were sleeping but…
3 The slide was busy but…
4 The lions had lots of food but….
5 The penguins slipped on the
   puddles but….

The sentences in this story have been linked by the wrong
words. Copy out each sentence putting in the right link word.
Use "and", "so" or "but". *(10 marks*

Zoe was a zoo keeper so she was not very good. She fed
carrots to the lions but meat to the rabbits. She never wore her
watch but she was always very late. Zoe loved animals but she
had lots of pets. She got better at her job but she won an
award.

Now write two linked sentences of your own using "and",
"so" or "but" to join two ideas into one long sentence.

Organisational devices

 **Key idea**

We can organise our writing in lots of different ways. When writing instructions we use boxes, bullet points, lists and numbers to make them clear. For example:

> Making an Easter Card. Cut out an egg shape. Stick it onto the front of your card. Fold the card in half and write your message inside.

It would look better like this:

> How to Make an Easter Card
>
> 1 Cut out an egg shape.
> 2 Stick it onto the front of your card.
> 3 Fold the card in half.
> 4 Write your message inside.

Try it out! • • • • • • • • • • • • • • • • • • •

★ **Top Tip**
Instructions often start with a verb as they are telling you to do something.

Write out these instructions for cleaning your teeth. Use numbers or letters to organise your writing. Use pictures to show what to do at each point. *(6 marks)*

How to Clean Your Teeth.

Get out your toothbrush. Put toothpaste on it. Wet your brush. Clean your teeth. Rinse your brush and your mouth. Put your brush away.

These instructions have got mixed up. Copy them out using numbers or boxes to make them clear. *(6 marks)*

How to Make Toast

Take the toast out of the toaster. Put a slice of bread in the toaster. Put on butter or jam. Wait for a few minutes. The toast will pop out when it's ready. Press down the button.

Here is a set of instructions for having a bath. Finish them off and order them on your page using numbers, letters, arrows, boxes or pictures to make them clear. *(18 marks)*

Have the Perfect Bath!
Put in the …
Turn on …
Add some …
Make sure the water is …
Put in some …
Turn off …
Check the …
Carefully, get into …
Enjoy your …!

Now write three more instructions about carefully getting out of the bath, pulling out the plug and getting dry.

Question marks

🔑 Key idea

A question mark tells the reader that a question is being asked. It comes at the end of a sentence which is a question.

> When will the plane land?

The question mark is used instead of a full stop.

The sentence is asking when the plane will land.

Try it out! ·

> ### ⭐ Top Tip
>
> Remember that you don't need to put a full stop after a question mark. Question marks have a full stop built in.

Copy out these five questions adding a question mark to the end of each one.

(2 marks for each correct answer)

1   Is this the airport
2   Where is the café
3   Can I see your ticket
4   Have you got your passport
5   Are those your bags

Keep practising!

Some of these sentences are questions. Write out the five questions and add a question mark to the end of each one.

(2 marks for each correct answer)

The door is shut.

It's seven o'clock.

Where is the exit.

Put on your seat belt.

Is your drink hot.

Where is my bag.

The plane is very big.

What is your name.

When do we arrive.

This is the alarm.

Take up the challenge!

Imagine you are going to interview an air steward. Think of five questions that you would like to ask them. Write each question down. Remember to put a question mark at the end. Use the words below to help you.

(2 marks for each correct answer)

How did you …

Where do you …

What is your favourite …

Is your job …

Would you …

Now write two more questions of your own. Remember to end each one with a question mark.

Assessment 1

unit 11

What's my ending?

Write out each sentence. Put in the missing capital letters, full stops or question marks. *(1 mark for each correct answer)*

1 amy was running for the bus
2 did you see the film
3 my puppy has a red collar
4 how did you do that
5 the cake was very nice
6 the snow melted away
7 are you going on holiday
8 the pen has run dry
9 did she hear the noise
10 the box was full of books

 Top Tip
Look back at Units 4, 5 and 10 to remind you! Remember that you don't need a full stop after a question mark.

Make sense!

Write out this story so that it makes sense. The word order is wrong. *(2 marks for each correct sentence)*

 ALERT
Say the sentences quietly to yourself to help you to work out the correct word order.

It raining was. Adam reading was his book. He out of looked the window. He puddle a big saw. Adam put wellingtons his on. He out went and big puddle in the splashed!

22

What a muddle!

Write out these sentences swapping the subject and the object.

They have got mixed up. *(1 mark for each correct sentence)*

Do it like this:

The cake ate a man = The man ate a cake.

1 The car got into the king.
2 The ball kicked a footballer.
3 A tunnel went through the train.
4 Some hats wore children.
5 The tree climbed the monkey.
6 The bone picked up the dog.
7 Stripes have zebras.
8 The laugh made us clown.

Exclamation marks

 Key idea

We use an exclamation mark to show excitement, surprise, danger or when someone in a story is shouting, excited or surprised. We also use them to show when something is loud.

BOOM!

Look out!

It was a giant spider!

The exclamation mark comes at the end of the sentence.

Try it out! •

> ⭐ **Top Tip**
> You do not need a full stop after an exclamation mark.

Copy out these sentences, adding an exclamation mark at the end of each one.

(2 marks for each correct sentence)

1   The Fair came to town.
2   The Big Wheel was very high.
3   One of the signs said DANGER.
4   The Ghost Train was scary.
5   Help.

Five of these eight sentences need an exclamation mark. Write them out and add an exclamation mark to them.

(2 marks for each correct answer)

!

ALERT
Remember that only five of them need an exclamation mark! Read them carefully.

It was David's special day.

David's mum had a surprise for him.

David got up and went downstairs.

He had some toast.

We're going to the Fair.

David went on every ride.

David's mum sat down.

David was so happy.

Here is the rest of the story about David's trip to the Fair. Copy it out and add in the five missing exclamation marks. *(10 marks)*

THE GHOST TRAIN!

David paid his money and sat in the car, soon it set off into the darkness. David saw a giant spider. Then he saw a ghost. David was very scared. David's mum waited for him outside. When the ride was over, he was so glad to be back with his mum.

Now write about three more scary things that David saw in the Ghost Train. Remember to use exclamation marks!

Commas

Key idea

A comma is used to give a short pause in a sentence. It breaks up a longer sentence into smaller parts. It can be used to make a sentence more exciting!

> Suddenly, there was a huge spider!

A pair of commas can be used to add extra information into a sentence.

> Davina was in Class 3.
>
> =
>
> Davina, who was six years old, was in Class 3.

The extra information has been added to the sentence using two commas.

Try it out! •

Write out these sentences adding a comma where you see /. *(2 marks for each correct sentence)*

1 Suddenly / they were inside the spooky room!
2 The door creaked / then slammed shut!
3 Just then / a bat appeared!
4 All at once / the lights went out!
5 Finally / they managed to escape!

Use two commas to add in the extra information.

For example:

The house (which had a spooky room in it) was next to Davina's.

=

The house, which had a spooky room in it, was next to Davina's.

(2 marks for each correct sentence)

1   Davina (who lived next door) wanted to go inside.
2   The key (which was very old) was found in a flower pot.
3   The room (which had been locked for 3 years) was now opened.
4   The walls (although quite dusty) still looked like new.
5   Even Davina (who was really quite brave) felt rather scared!

Take up the challenge! •

Copy out the story putting in the ten missing commas. *(10 marks)*

Davina (who lived in East Street) was a very brave girl. She looked into the spooky room / but it was very dark inside. Suddenly / she felt a cold wind and heard a funny noise. Davina (who knew a lot about animals) had not heard this noise before. Something moved (rather quickly) over her head. It wasn't a ghost / it was a bat. A family of bats were living in the roof / there was no ghost!

Now write about how Davina felt when she knew there was no ghost! Try to use three commas in your writing.

Speech marks

🔑 Key idea

We use **speech marks** to show when someone is speaking.

"My name is Fred," said the robot.

What the robot said is put inside speech marks.

Try it out! •

Write out Fred the Robot's instructions, adding speech marks.

(5 marks)

1   Turn on the computer.
2   Go to the control room.
3   Watch the screen.
4   Set the controls.
5   Get ready for landing.

Keep practising!

Write out this speech putting in the speech marks. *(10 marks)*

My name is Fred, said the Robot.
Where have we landed? asked the Captain.
We are on Mars, replied Fred.
Open the doors! cried the Captain.
I obey! replied Fred.

Top Tip

Question marks and exclamation marks go inside the speech marks.

Take up the challenge!

Fred the Robot talked to ROSE, the on-board computer. Add in the speech marks to what they said. The first one has been done for you. *(15 marks)*

"Are your screens working? asked Fred. Yes, replied ROSE, I am ready to carry out some jobs for you. Good, said Fred. What is the name of this planet? It is called Titan 5, ROSE said quickly. Oh no! cried Fred. This is a prison planet!

Now carry on the speech with ROSE's reply!

Speech bubbles

🔑 Key idea

A speech bubble is used to show who is speaking and what they have said. Speech bubbles are used in pictures, cartoons, posters and information texts.

What the mouse says is put inside a speech bubble. We do not use speech marks inside a speech bubble.

Try it out! •

⭐ Top Tip

Remember, you do not need speech marks inside a speech bubble!

Write each of these speeches inside speech bubbles. Draw each character's head to show who is talking. *(2 marks for each correct speech bubble)*

"Have you seen the cat?" said the mouse.
"I'm coming to get you!" said the cat.
"I can run faster than you!" said the dog.
"I can see you down there!" said the bird.
"Who took my cheese?" said the farmer.

Copy the picture and write in what each character might be saying. *(10 marks)*

When two characters say more than one thing to each other a second speech bubble is drawn below for their next speech. Put in the speech and carry it on. *(10 marks)*

"I am faster than you!" said the dog.
"No you're not!" said the cat.
"................." said the dog.
"................." said the cat.
"................." said the dog.

Now try writing speech bubbles for a lion and a crocodile!

unit 16

Ways of presenting text - BLOCK CAPITALS

🔑 Key idea

We sometimes use BLOCK CAPITALS in our writing to show that something is important, scary, exciting or dangerous. It can also show that someone is shouting or we are giving an instruction or warning.

The door was marked DANGER!

"Don't go in THERE!"

"It's YOUR turn!"

The word we want to stress is in BLOCK CAPITALS.

Try it out! •

Write these out using BLOCK CAPITALS to show that they are important. *(2 marks for each correct sentence)*

1 Do not drink.
2 Slippery floor.
3 Do not swim.
4 No diving.
5 Falling rocks.

Keep practising!

Write these out using BLOCK CAPITALS
for the important word in each sentence.

(2 marks for each correct sentence)

1   The sea can be dangerous.
2   I'm lost!
3   That coffee is hot!
4   It's your birthday!
5   I'm cold!

Top Tip

Only one word in each
sentence needs to be in
block capitals.

Take up the challenge!

Write out this short story with five of the words in
BLOCK CAPITALS. Look carefully to decide
which words. *(10 marks)*

Anya burst into Robert's bedroom shouting,
"Happy Birthday!"
Robert looked at all his presents tied onto
balloons. "Wow!" he thought to himself. All
of a sudden one of the balloons went
bang! "Sorry!" shouted Anya and
they both laughed.

Now write two more sentences
with at least one word in
block capitals.

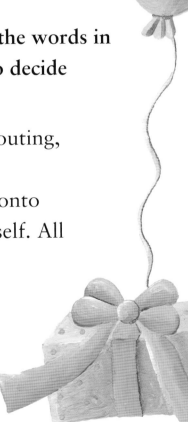

33

unit 17 Assessment 2

What is missing?

Write out this speech, making each line correct.

Look back to Unit 14 to give you some clues! *(10 marks)*

That's my toy! shouted Tom.

"No it's not, it's mine! replied Moira.

"It's mine because it has _____ ," said Tom.

"You're making it up!" cried _____

Oh no, I'm not! screamed Tom.

Now both of you make friends. It's ADAM's toy! said Mum.

Exclamations!

Write out this speech adding in the exclamation marks.

There are five to add. *(2 marks for each exclamation mark)*

"Wow" shouted Tom. "Look at that"

"It's a balloon" exclaimed Moira. "A hot air balloon has landed in our garden"

"I think I'm lost" shouted the pilot. Tom and Moira laughed.

Place those commas!

Read these sentences carefully. Put in the missing commas. *(2 marks for each correct sentence)*

 **Top Tip**
Read the sentences quietly to yourself to see where the commas should go.

1 Pass me my cup of coffee please.
2 Pick up your jumper Tom.
3 What's the matter Moira?
4 No I don't want a drink.
5 Don't do that Adam!

Now write two sentences which use pairs of commas to add extra information.

Commas in lists

 Key idea

Commas are used to separate items in a list.

> Jamie bought a ball, a comic, a chew bar, a bag of crisps and a drink.

The last two items in a list are joined by "and" to show it is the end of this list.

Try it out! ·

 Top Tip

There are no commas just before the "and".

Write out these lists adding in the commas.

(2 marks for each correct sentence)

1 Joe put his books jumper a pear and his pens into his bag.

2 When Joe got to the pool he took out his towel trunks swimming cap and his goggles.

3 Joe put on his boots socks shorts and shirt for the football match.

4 Joe ate a cake a bar of chocolate a choc ice and a bun at the party.

5 When Joe got home he put away his coat shoes books and bag.

Look at these lists carefully. Write them out adding the
commas, plus the "and" between the last two items. *(10 marks)*

1 Joe's paint was red blue green yellow.
2 Joe played football with Ajay Moira Ben Jaswinder.
3 Joe saw a monkey a lion a seal a giraffe a bear at the Zoo.

Take up the challenge! •

Finish these lists adding in the commas, plus the "and" for the
last two items. *(10 marks)*

On my desk I have a pencil ……... ……... …. ……...
In my bag I've got my reading book ……... ……... …. ……...
In my bedroom I've got my bed ……... ……... …. ……...
My favourite colours are ……... ……... …. ……...
My favourite foods are ……... ……... …. ……...

**Now ask a friend about their favourite colours and food and
write down their list using commas plus "and".**

Regular past tense

unit 19

Key idea

We use the past tense to say when something has already happened. Many verbs make the past tense by adding **ed**.

I play on the drums – it is happening now; it is the **present tense**.

I played on the drums – it happened some time ago; it is the **past tense**.

Try it out!

Write out this short story adding ed **to the verbs in bold.**

(2 marks for each correct sentence)

I **play** with Sophie. I **look** at lots of books with her. I **shout** to Sophie in the playground. We **watch** T.V. together. We **jump** in all the puddles!

Keep practising!

Put these sentences into the past by adding ed. *(2 marks for each correct sentence)*

!

ALERT
If a verb ends in "e" then drop the "e" and add "ed". dance = danced.

1 I **like** Sophie's party.
2 I **dance** at her disco.
3 I **smile** at everyone.
4 I **giggle** at the clown.
5 I **wave** goodbye to Sophie at the end.

Take up the challenge!

Write this list of jobs in the past tense. *(2 marks for each correct sentence)*

1 I wash the car with my dad.
2 I polish the lights.
3 I use the hose-pipe.
4 I clean the windscreen.
5 I wipe the mirror.

Now write two more jobs you could do at home using the past tense.

Tricky past tenses!

🔑 Key idea

Not all verbs add **ed** to put them in the past. Verbs which do not add **ed** are called **irregular** verbs.

I **go** to the shop = I **went** to the shop.

We can check by adding **ed**. If it doesn't sound right, then it must be an irregular verb.

Try it out! •

Match up these verbs with their past tenses. *(2 marks for each correct answer)*

see	eat	fly	give	sit
gave	saw	sat	flew	ate

Finish these sentences. Choose the right past tense! *(2 marks for each correct answer)*

1   A magician _____ to school. (comed/came)
2   He _____ a chosen card. (found/finded)
3   He _____ a big, black hat. (weared/wore)
4   I _____ his magic wand. (holded/held)
5   We all _____ and clapped. (sat/sitted)

Take up the challenge! ●

Write out this story putting it into the past tense. *(2 marks for each correct answer)*

Marvo the Magician (come) to school. We all (go) into the Hall to see his show. I (run) to the front to help him. I (sing) the magic words and a dove (fly) out of his hat!

Now write two more sentences using irregular past tenses to say what Marvo the Magician did next!

Does my sentence make sense?

🔑 Key idea

Sentences must make sense and all their parts must work together.

> The Queen wore his tiara.

This sentence doesn't make sense as the Queen is wearing **his** tiara. Each part of the sentence must "agree". Check that verbs and personal pronouns (he, she) agree so that your sentences make sense.

> The Queen was wearing her tiara.

We must also check that the subject and the verb "agree".

> The Queen were cross = The Queen was cross.

Try it out! ●

Write out these sentences, correcting the mistakes! *(2 marks for each correct sentence)*

1   The Queen picked up his handbag.
2   The King was scratching her bald head.
3   The King loved its castle.
4   The Prince was carrying their sword.
5   The Princess had ribbons in his hair.

Choose the correct verb to complete these sentences. *(2 marks for each correct answer)*

1   The King _____ hot.   (were/was)
2   "Here you _____ ," (is/are) said the Queen.
3   She _____ (give/gave) him some cool water.
4   The King _____ (drank/drink) the water.
5   The King and Queen _____ (was/were) happy.
6   They _____ (go/went) into the castle.

Take up the challenge! •

Write out this story, making sure it makes sense! *(8 marks)*

The Prince wanted to ride on its horse. He see the King, but he said, "No!" The Prince were cross, so he run out of the castle!

Finish the story about the Prince and his horse. Check that your sentences make sense!

unit 22 Question words

Key idea

When we write a question, we often start with a question word. A question word asks a question all by itself.

Who said that?

Who? Why? When? Where? What? How?

We use questions in our writing to make it more interesting.

Try it out!

Write out these sentences, putting in the question word at the start. *(2 marks for each correct sentence)*

Who	What	Why	When	Where

1 _____ are you crying?

2 _____ day is it?

3 _____ is your house?

4 _____ knows the answer?

5 _____ is it bedtime?

Why am I here?

Keep practising!

Sort these into questions about Who? When? Where? Make three lists in your book. *(2 marks for each correct answer)*

Is that Bill?

Are you at the park?

What time shall we meet?

Did you say that?

Did I leave it here?

Take up the challenge!

Write questions for these answers. *(2 marks for each correct question)*

1   I am seven years old.
2   I have one brother but no sisters.
3   My favourite colour is green.
4   Yes, I do like fish.
5   I have two cats.

Now write two more questions.

Assessment 3

Check this out

Copy these sentences putting in the missing capital letters, full stops and question marks. *(0.5 mark for each correction)*

1 Have you seen amit
2 Moira and david looked everywhere
3 what time did the game start
4 where did you look
5 is he near the gate
6 david and moira were worried.
7 when did you last see him
8 Moira found amit hiding in a tree
9 amit and moira laughed.
10 what happened to David

In the past

Write these verbs in the past tense. *(1 mark for each correct answer)*

play= _____   call= _____

pull= _____   paint= _____

knock= _____   push= _____

watch= _____   look= _____

A tense moment

Finish this story writing it out in the past tense. *(1 mark for each correct answer)*

One cold night, Little Owl (go) _____ to see his old friend Big Owl. He (fly) _____ over the tall trees to Big Owl's house. The two owls (sing)_____ songs together and then they (eat) _____ a huge meal of mouse pie and gravy. They (drink) _____ pop and both (have) _____ a great time.

Does it agree?

Choose the correct word to finish each sentence. *(1 mark for each correct answer)*

1   The gentleman wore _____ suit. (his/her)
2   The lady wore _____ dress. (his/her)
3   The guests _____ excited. (was/were)
4   The party_____very big. (was/were)
5   There _____ lots of drinks at _____ party. (was/were/their/mine)

Glossary

capital letter
A sentence always starts with a capital letter. Names of people, places, titles, days and months all begin with a capital letter. *I went to London on Monday.*

comma
A comma is a punctuation mark, which tells the reader to pause. It also separates items in a list. *Please, can you help me? Adam bought apples, pears, grapes and bananas from the shop.*

exclamation
An exclamation is a sentence that shows that we are excited, shocked, surprised or feel something strongly. It always ends with an exclamation mark. *Look out!*

object
The object of a sentence is the person or thing that has something done to them. *Adam kicked the **ball**.*

question
A question is something we ask when we want to know something. We often use a question word to start our sentence, like "Who", "What", "Where" or "When". Questions always end with a question mark. *Have you shut the door?*

sentence
A sentence is a group of words which make sense and convey an idea. It should begin with a capital letter and often ends with a full stop.

subject
The subject of a sentence is the person or thing that is active in the sentence. *Moira watched T.V.*

tense
The tense of a verb tells *when* the action taking place. The *past* tense is used when something has already happened. Regular verbs make the past by adding –ed (play = *played*). Irregular verbs have their own way of making the past tense (go = *went*).

word order
Words must be placed carefully in a sentence so that they make sense.
David was late for school.
Was David late for school?